SWEET MEMORIES

SWEET MEMORIES

A Gingerbread Family Scrapbook

● ● ● ● ● ● ●

Sally Ryder Brady   Sarah Brady Underwood   Sara Pinto   Luciana Frigerio

BLOOMSBURY

Published by Bloomsbury USA, New York
Distributed to the trade by Holtzbrinck Publishers

All papers used by Bloomsbury USA are natural, recyclable products made from wood grown in well-managed forests. The manufacturing processes conform to the environmental regulations of the country of origin.

Library of Congress Cataloging-in-Publication Data

Sweet memories : a gingerbread family scrapbook / Sara Pinto . . . [et al.].—1st U.S. ed.
p. cm.
ISBN-13: 978-1-59691-044-7
ISBN-10: 1-59691-044-5
1. Family life—Humor. 2. Gingerbread—Humor. I. Pinto, Sara.

PN6231.F3.S94 2006
818'.60208—dc22
2005044802

First U.S. Edition 2006

2 4 6 8 10 9 7 5 3 1

Designed and typeset by John Candell
Printed in China by South China Printing Co.

To everyone who has ever
overworked their dough

Blind with passion, Fred and Ginger were unaware of the perils
that lay ahead on their long voyage.

Uh-oh! Who invited the bachelor party entertainment to the wedding?

Mr. and Mrs. Holiday Treat
Request the Honor of
Your Presence at the
Wedding
of their Daughter, Ginger
to Frederick G. Bread III
Saturday, July 3rd
Our Lady of Immaculate
Confection Church

Reception to Follow

Fred and Ginger Bread

DISCREET BACHELOR PARTIES

THE HONEY-B... GIRL...

UNDO THE GINGER SNAPS! (COSTS EXTRA)

DEVOTED 3rd BEST WEDDING BAND IN THE TRISTATES

BAKED BOYZ BAND

ROCK YOUR SILVER BALLS OFF AND SHAKE THOSE SPRINKLES!

GINGER TREAT &
ANTI-NAUSEA
DR. KNEAD   Rx

Exhausted from her wedding night, Ginger fell asleep on
the beach and burned to a crisp.

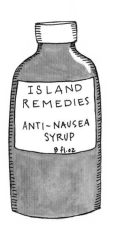

Ginger didn't mind moving into Fred's bachelor pad, but the cracker
neighbors were something she hadn't bargained on.

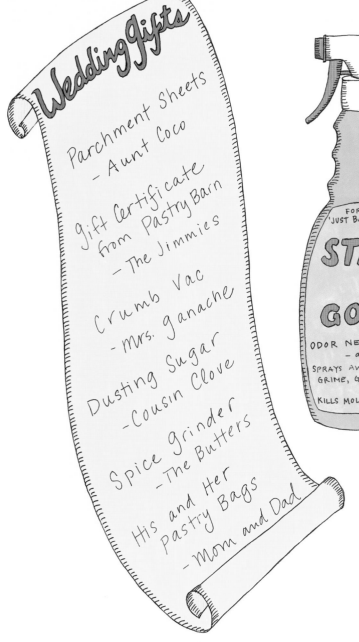

Wedding Gifts

Parchment Sheets
— Aunt Coco

Gift Certificate
from Pastry Barn
— The Jimmies

Crumb Vac
— Mrs. Ganache

Dusting Sugar
— Cousin Clove

Spice Grinder
— The Butters

His and Her
Pastry Bags
— Mom and Dad

FOR THAT
'JUST BAKED' SMELL

STALE B GONE

ODOR NEUTRALIZER
— also —
SPRAYS AWAY GERMS,
GRIME, GRIT + GREASE
—
KILLS MOLD ON CONTACT

YOU'RE INVITED!

WHAT: Tupperware Party!!

WHERE: 87 POTHOLDER PLACE

WHEN: 7 pm

WHO: Ginger Bread, hostess

WHY: BECAUSE WE ALL WANT
TO STAY FRESH AND
LOOK OUR BEST!

JAR, SWEET JAR

R BREAD Rx
TI-NAUSEA
ARANOIA
IC ATTACKS
NEAD, MD

At the last minute, the new neonatal convection oven at the birthing center saved little Fred from being half-baked.

FIVE-POINTED STAR

SIDEWAYS PLANK

HEAD STAND

SHAVASANA

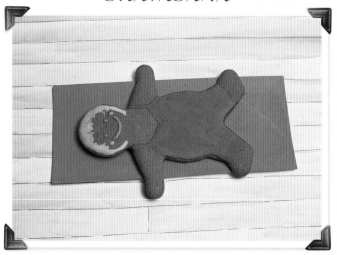

Ginger tried Jazzercise before discovering the unusual flexibility
that would transform her into a yoga star.

The dot-com boom made it possible for Fred and Ginger to move to
Pepper Ridge Farm Estates, an upscale gated community.

The children couldn't believe their luck—the nice sheep had more Halloween candy in his car, but then they remembered the rule about strangers.

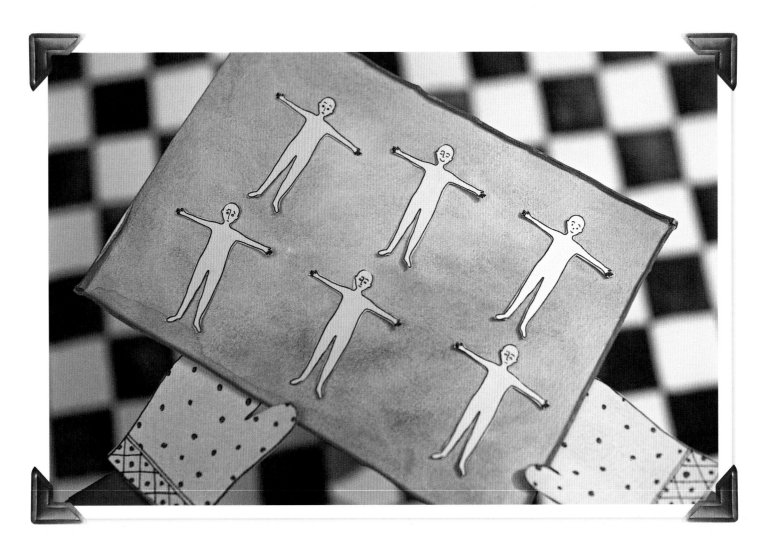

Every December, Grandma, Ginger, and the children baked
holiday people together—it's a family tradition!

HOLIDAY PEOPLE COOKIES

1 C. blood
2 C. bonemeal
4 C. fat (can substitute cellulite)
pinch of gray matter

Mix, roll and cut.
Bake until dry and wrinkly.
Sprinkle with dandruff and crushed nuts.

Seasons
greetings
from
The Breads

EAT ME,
IT'S
X-MAS

While Fred was away opening up the office in China, milk was
not the only thing the green-eyed milkman delivered.

FORTUNE COOKIE 500

BREAD RISES TO 'SUGAR DADDY' IN THE BOARDROOM

No. 52

LOTUS AIR
BOARDING PASS
PASSENGER: BREAD, F. FLIGHT No. 7
MEAL: NO · SNACK: NO · MOVIE: NONE
HOT TOWELS: NO · DRINKS: NO · TO
OXYGEN: COSTS EXTRA · EARP
RESTRICTIONS: NO SHOES ALLO
NO HAND GRENADES, KNIVES
FIRECRACKERS, CHRISTMAS CR
NO CANDY THERMOMETE

FRED BREAD OPENS SHANGHAI OFFICE
ODY
LIMBS
REFUND
NO TIES
TWEEZERS
SWORDS
OF ANY KIND

COMPANY TO GO PUBLIC

BREAD CONSIDERS HOSTESS TAKEOVER OF DINGDONG CO.

SAY IT IN MANDARIN

8 HOURS TO FLUENT CHINESE

我一定不欺骗你

DONT FORGET OUR OTHER BOOKS IN THIS SERIES

ANCIENT CHINESE SAYING: DONT CRY OVER SPILT MILK - NO GOOD IN YOUR CASE

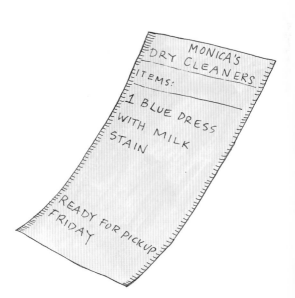

MONICA'S DRY CLEANERS
ITEMS:
1 BLUE DRESS WITH MILK STAIN
READY FOR PICKUP FRIDAY

What made Baby Willy different were his green eyes,
permanent mustache, and insatiable appetite for milk.

With the dot-com bust, a new baby, and the mortgage,
Ginger started selling Merry Kay bake-up.

Fred and Ginger weren't sending Grandma and Grandpa to a "stale folks home"—it was an assifted-living community. There was a difference.

TODAY IS WEDNESDAY, JUNE 1st

YOU ARE AT CONTINUING CRISPNESS™ NURSING HOME

DAILY SCHEDULE

4:30 AM BREAKFAST

7:30 AM CRISPERCIZE IN THE REC. ROOM 'LET'S SWEAT!!'

8:30 AM CRAFTERS CIRCLE

10:30 AM LUNCH!

1:00 PM WALKER RACING WITH NURSE FOXY LOXY

3:00 PM GUEST SPEAKER IN COMMUNAL ROOM

4:00 PM SUPPER (AKA DINNER)

6:00 PM MOVIE: COCOAOON STARRING JESSICA CANDY

8:00 PM LIGHTS OUT

UPCOMING EVENTS

POTHOLDER WEAVING IS NOT JUST FOR KIDS!

JOIN OUR OWN NURSE FOXY LOXY AS SHE DEMONSTRATES THIS FASCINATING CRAFT. LOOPS PROVIDED. IN YEARS PAST, RESIDENTS HAVE DONATED POTHOLDERS TO THE LOCAL UMSO (UNWED MOTHERS STATE OVENS)

LIVING WITHOUT LIMBS

DR. REYNARD, HYPNOTHERAPIST, PRESENTS

SCRAPBOOK MAKING

TRANSFORM YOUR BANAL, MEDIOCRE PAST INTO AN EXCITING BOOK OF CREATIVE MEMORIES! PHOTOS WILL BE PROVIDED IF YOU'VE FORGOTTEN WHERE YOURS ARE. COURSE FEE $975. INCLUDES NOVELTY PAPERS, GLUE, PUNCH HOLES, CRAZY SCISSORS, RIBBON, CUTE QUOTES, ALBUM BOOKS, SCRATCH AND SNIFF STICKERS, YOUR OWN ORIGINAL IDEAS AND MUCH MORE

MENU

BREAKFAST:
PORRIDGE, PRUNE JUICE OR TOMATO JUICE

LUNCH:
CREAMED CORN, PRUNE JUICE OR PINEAPPLE JUICE

DINNER:
CREAMED CORN AND PORRIDGE SOUFFLE, PRUNE JUICE OR ARSENIC

At the Museum of Natural History, Ginger was horrified by
Gingibratus erectus wearing only his natural raisins.

MUSEUM of NATURAL HISTORY

VOL. 347

WHAT'S HAPPENING AT THE MUSEUM THIS WEEK

SCIENCE PROVES CHOCOLATE CHIP DNA = ELEPHANT DUNG

How STALE IS STALE? THE CARBON DATING GAME

UNRAVELING THE SECRETS OF OUR MAIN INGREDIENTS: COULD SCIENCE PROVE THE EXISTENCE OF A MASTER CHEF?

GRAY FOX AND BIG BAD WOLF SHARE MORE THAN AN UNCANNY RESEMBLANCE. WATCH THE DISSECTION OF A FOX AND WOLF BRAIN EVERY HOUR ON THE HOUR

VISIT THE CRO-MAGNON EXHIBIT ... NOW MORE LIFELIKE THAN EVER!

MUSEUM of NATURAL HISTORY
LIFETIME PASS

FRUCTOSE FREE PRESS

ADMINISTRATION BANS DOUGH FREEZING

MASSIVE PROTESTS PLANNED FOR WEEK

GET YOUR HANDS OFF MY DOUGH

STUDY FINDS TEENS LIKELY TO FREE BASE SUGAR

HIGH COURTS DECIDE STIFF PUNISHMENT FOR CANNIBALS

LOCAL MOTHER OUTRAGED AT INAPPROPRIATE RAISIN DISPLAY

"IT'S NOT HIDEOUS, IT'S HISTORY," MAINTAINS TOP BRASS AT MUSEUM

MUSEUM AWARDS MOTHER FREE LIFETIME PASSES FOR ENTIRE FAMILY

Museum Gift Shop

Authentic Raisin Reproduction Beachwear

Fred and Ginger were unaware of the risks inherent in
skiing when they booked the family vacation.

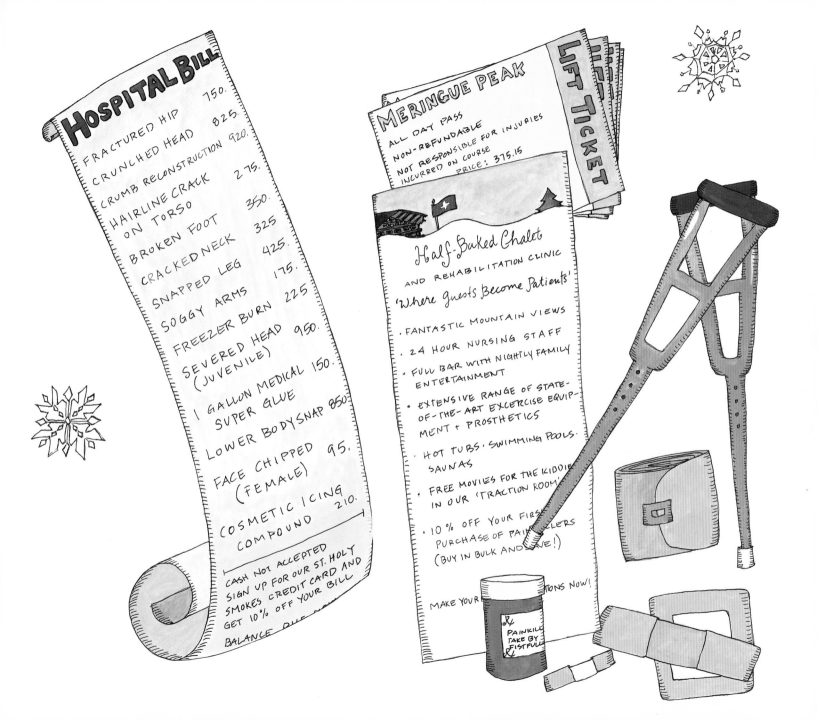

"This is for your own good, Cookie. You don't want to end up
going door to door selling bake-up, do you?"

Our Lady of Immaculate Confection
Catholic School
awards this diploma to:

Cookie Bread

Special commendation for Bravery and least amounts of visits to the Infirmary!

IC

Our Lady of
Immaculate Confection
CATHOLIC SCHOOL
PROUDLY PRESENTS THE 75TH

GRADUATING CLASS

PROGRAM

PROCESSION (SELF FLAGELLATION OPTIONAL)

COMMENCEMENT SPEAKER:

BETTY CRACKER
"DON'T PREJUDGE THE COOKIE CUTTER"

VALEDICTORIAN: COOKIE BREAD
"BRUTAL ABUSE OR TOUGH LOVE;
LOOK AT ME AND DECIDE"
– • –

COMMENCEMENT CEREMONIES LED BY
MOTHER SUPERIOR MARY MARGARET

CRUMB LAUDE

Even though it was in Fred Jr.'s genes to run, run, run,
a little extra boost never hurts.

Losing weight was an uphill battle: Cookie was entirely made of carbs.

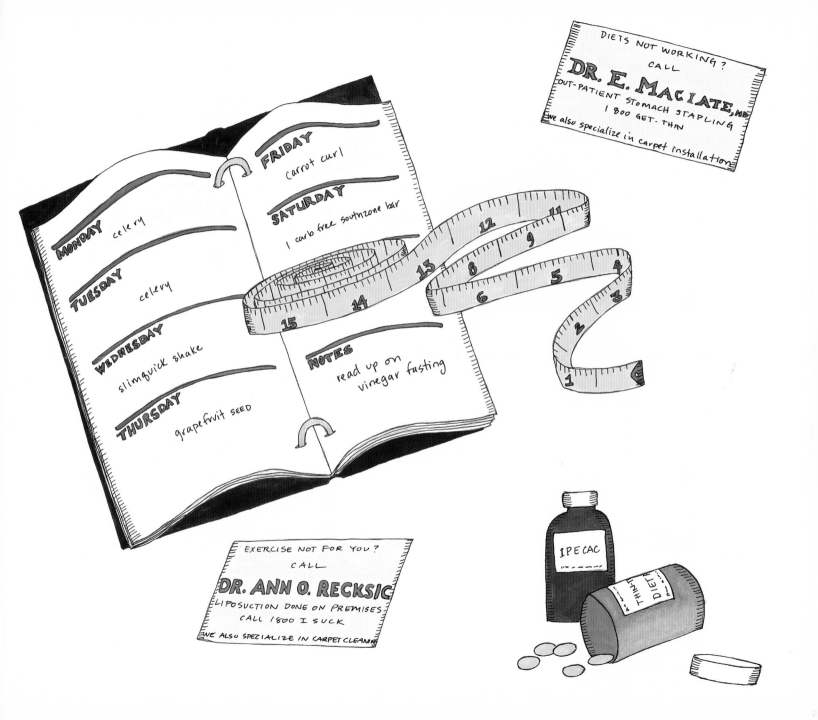

After saying good-bye, Grandma felt sure Grandpa's crumbmains
would be handled with care and respect.

Guests
Gigi LeSweet Olivia Sweet
Galen Gateau Max Munchie
Zachary Sucre Aidan Amaretto
Lucca Linzer Dr. D. Wing

Guests
Major Douglas Wattermire
Mrs. Macadamia
Mr. Woodrow Long
Cecilia Dough William F.

OBITUARIES

DESSERT DREAM, AZ
SEPT. 22 — HERB BREAD,
86, beloved half-marathon
runner, died here Tuesday
at Continuing Crispness Assifted Living.
The cause was a massive congestive crumble.

Bread ran the famous 20k Candy
Classic for thirty consecutive years, wir
every race, to become a legend in k
own time. Bread has been the subj
of many books on running, inc
the children's favorite, "Run! Run! R

Bread was also a beloved m
coach. He retired ten years a
focus on his second vocation,
to keep the fox-hunt alive in thi

He is survived by his wife
his son, Fred and three grand
Services will be held at the Cal

Calm Repose
CRUMBATORIUM

· TRADITIONAL OPEN
  CASKET SERVICES
· GENTLE CRUMBATION
· UNIQUE SELECTION
  OF URNS FOR YOUR
  LOVED ONE'S CRUMBAINS—
  INCLUDING OUR EVER-
  POPULAR ANT-PROOF
  URN.
· ALLOW OUR EXPERIENCED
  AND PROFESSIONAL
  STAFF TO HELP EASE
  UNCERTAINTIES AND
  DISCOMFORT.

KEEP THIS FREE MAGNET
AS OUR GIFT TO YOU

To celebrate their twenty-fifth anniversary, Fred and Ginger
returned to the place where it all began.

THE END.

RECIPE FOR ABOUT FOUR DOZEN ILL-FATED GINGERBREAD PEOPLE

Do not make these on a rainy day or they will get the bends

2 cups molasses
1½ cups packed brown sugar
½ cup unsalted butter
½ cup shortening
1 tablespoon baking soda

½ cup boiling water
6½ cups plus 2 tablespoons flour
3 tablespoons ground ginger
2 tablespoons ground cinnamon
1 tablespoon ground cloves

Combine first four ingredients in 4-quart saucepan. Stir over medium heat until sugar dissolves. Meanwhile, dissolve baking soda in water and add to molasses mixture. Mix flour, ginger, cinnamon, and cloves. Add to mixture in saucepan, stirring vigorously until completely blended. Form dough into 4 rectangles. Wrap each in plastic. Chill.

Preheat oven to 275°, and bring dough to room temperature. Butter cookie sheets or line with parchment. Dust rolling pin and countertop with flour, and roll out one rectangle of dough no thicker than a dime. Cut into shapes and place on buttered sheets. Bake for 10 minutes. Let cookies cool for a few minutes before removing to wire rack to cool.

We used King Arthur white icing mix, as well as King Arthur colored sugars and sprinkles. Or, if you prefer, you can make your own icing:

PLAIN ICING

1 cup confectioners' sugar
1 to 2 tablespoons heavy cream
1 teaspoon vanilla
food coloring

Mix sugar, cream, and vanilla to consistency of slightly runny pudding. Spoon into as many little cups as you have different colors of food coloring, and add color to icing in cups. Paint cookies with a paintbrush and decorate with sprinkles, dragées, colored sugars, etc. Store cookies in a tin lined with waxed paper. These cookies will keep for years when tightly stored.